YOUR KNOWLEDGE HAS VALUE

- We will publish your bachelor's and master's thesis, essays and papers

- Your own eBook and book - sold worldwide in all relevant shops

- Earn money with each sale

Upload your text at www.GRIN.com
and publish for free

Regina Seiwald

Future. Meaning and Form

GRIN Publishing

Bibliographic information published by the German National Library:

The German National Library lists this publication in the National Bibliography; detailed bibliographic data are available on the Internet at http://dnb.dnb.de .

Imprint:

Copyright © 2008 GRIN Verlag GmbH
Print and binding: Books on Demand GmbH, Norderstedt Germany
ISBN: 978-3-656-95415-6

This book at GRIN:

http://www.grin.com/en/e-book/89562/future-meaning-and-form

GRIN - Your knowledge has value

Since its foundation in 1998, GRIN has specialized in publishing academic texts by students, college teachers and other academics as e-book and printed book. The website www.grin.com is an ideal platform for presenting term papers, final papers, scientific essays, dissertations and specialist books.

Visit us on the internet:

http://www.grin.com/

http://www.facebook.com/grincom

http://www.twitter.com/grin_com

Proseminar Paper

Future

- Meaning and Form -

University of Innsbruck

Humanities

English and American Studies

Third Term

December 2007

Proseminar Language Awareness III.

Winter Term 2007/08

Index of Contents

= = = = = = = = = =

Introduction

This Proseminar paper is about "Future – Meaning and Form", following the presentation held in the Awareness III. course in winter term 2007/08. In order to analyse the different forms and meanings of the various future concepts, there are several English Grammar books providing useful theoretical information.

The first part of the paper serves as a theoretical overview. In this section the different future concepts are analysed and the meaning of the different tenses is dissected. The second part consists of the practical part. It illustrates where and why the different future concepts are used in different examples. It also shows how the rules in the theoretical part apply to the practical examples like dialogues and full texts.

I.   Theoretical Part

A. Preface

In English, like in all Germanic languages, there is no simple future tense. The futurity of an action is expressed either by using a word which expresses a future action, e.g. I drive to London *in two days,* or by utilising an auxiliary construction that combines a definite present tense verb with the stem of this verb which illustrates the actual action of the sentence.

The English future tense was established during the period of 300 years, between 1066 and 1350. During that time, Anglo-Norman was the official language of the British Isles. Unlike English, Norman is a Romance Language, which does have a simple future tense.

In the course of the study of the English future concepts, one has to make a difference between spoken and written language. As spoken language is used more often than written language, the used future tense differs.

This abstract is based on the internet article from
<http://en.wikipedia.org/wiki/Future_tense>
on December 22nd, 2007

B. Will/Shall Future

Will/Shall is used to ask or give information in cases where there is no reason to use a present verb-form. It is also used to predict the future when we want to say what we guess, think or calculate will happen. The will/shall future is formed with will/shall and simple verb form.

Will is more commonly used in modern British English, but will and shall are used with no difference. They are interchangeable. (Downing – Locke 359)

Will/shall is used in spontaneous decisions announced at the time of making them without a previous plan. (Hewings 18)

e.g. I'm starving. I **will eat** a sandwich.
→ I feel hungry and at the same moment I make the announcement that I will eat something.

The will/shall future is also used when you are expressing your own opinion about the future happenings and for forecasts. (18)

e.g. Tomorrow **will be** dry, some clouds in the afternoon.
→ The weather forecast has some evidence for it, but it is not absolutely clear that the weather will be dry.

It is utilised in formal announcements like newspaper articles or formal pieces of writing. (18)

e.g. President Bush **will give** a speech in New York next week.

→ Bush has announced to hold a speech and as it is written in a newspaper article, the will future is used.

C. Going to Future

Present verb-forms are often used to talk about the future. We commonly use going to if we talk about decisions, plans or firm intentions, especially in an informal style. Be is put into the correct verb form to agree with the subject, followed by going to and the simple verb form. (18)

The going to future is used for plans or intentions. It is announced after it has been decided if no active steps were taken. (18)

    e.g. I **am going** to apply for university next week.

    → I have already decided to apply but did not fill in the application form.

It is also utilised if predictions are based on evidence, so one has to interpret concrete signs. (18)

    e.g. Look at the yellowish sky! It **is going** to hail.

    → I can see that the sky is yellowish. The logical consequence is that it is going to hail.

D. Present Continuous

The Present Continuous, or Present Progressive, is used when we want to talk about future fixed plans or personal arrangements. The time, date and/or place is often given. It is formed with be in the correct verb form to agree with the verb and the simple verb form with –ing at the end. (20)

For future arrangements, which are more than just a plan, the Present Continuous is used. Something has been already arranged.

    e.g. I **am meeting** the manager of Liebherr Africa tomorrow.

    → I have arranged the meeting some time ago.

The Present Continuous is also used for actions which are just starting.

    e.g. I **am quitting** my job next week.

    → I have already told my boss that I am quitting the job next week.

E. Comparison of Structure

To talk about the same future event we can often use more than one structure to talk about it. Present forms emphasise present ideas like plans, certainty and intention. When we are not emphasising present ideas we prefer will/shall. (Hewings 18; Swan – Walter 135)

e.g. Next week **is going to be** different. Mum promised it.

→ This is a present intention.

e.g. Next week **will be** different.

→ It could also stay the same.

If future events have some present reality, present forms are used.

e.g. I **am meeting** my aunt next week

→ There is an arrangement.

e.g. I wonder if he **will recognise** me.

→ This is no present idea.

F. Present Simple with Future Reference

The Present Simple is sometimes used to talk about the future, mostly when we talk about schedules, routines and timetables. It is constructed with the simple verb form. In the third case, i.e. he/she/it, –s is put at the end of the verb. (20)

The present simple is used for definite schedules or timetables. These are facts which are true to everyone. (20)

e.g. The plane to London **leaves** at 2:30 p.m.

→ It is a definite schedule and it is true to everyone.

This time concept is also used after time conjunctions. (20)

e.g. I will get back to you when Cathy **arrives**.

→ As when is a time conjunction, the following verb is in present simple.

In other cases the present simple is not used in main clauses to talk about the future. (20)

e.g. Anna **is coming** for a drink next evening.

→ NOT Anna ~~comes~~ for a drink next evening. This is not true to everyone.

G. Future Perfect

The Future Perfect is constructed with <u>will have</u> and the <u>past participle.</u> (Downing – Locke 360)

It is used when events are completed by a certain time. (Hewings 22)

e.g. She **will have completed** her work by next Wednesday.

→ By this time she has finished her work and therefore it is completed.

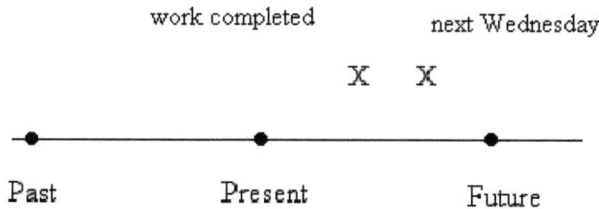

H. Future Continuous

The Future Continuous is formed with <u>will be</u>, followed by the <u>simple verb form</u> and <u>–ing</u> at the end. Unlike the simple future forms, Future Perfect and Future Continuous are usually interchangeable. (Downing – Locke 359)

The Future Continuous is used if activities are in progress at a given time. Emphasis is put on the activity that has been fixed. (Hewings 22)

e.g. This time next week I **will be flying** to Pattaya.

→ The emphasis is put on the duration or progress of the flight.

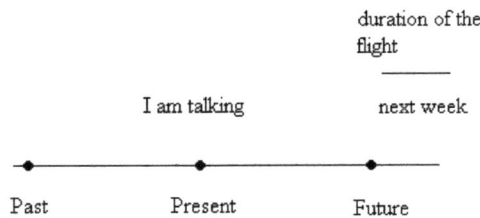

The Future Continuous is used if one wants to express neutral reference. This does not imply a threat, a decision or a promise. (22)

e.g. We **will be discussing** this issue next month.

→ This is a neutral reference .

I. Adverbial Time Clauses

Time Clauses begin with words related to time, like <u>after, as soon as, before, if, since, until, when and while</u>. When the main clause consists of a future concept, the adverbial clause must always be in the present tense. (Swan – Walter 137)

e.g. **As soon as** I come home I **will give** you a call.

→ This is a conditional clause. I first have to get home and afterwards I can give you a call.

If and <u>when</u> can be followed by <u>will</u> in direct or indirect questions. (137)

    e.g. **When will** you see them again?

    → When is followed by will as this is a direct question.

J. Idiomatic Expressions

    Futurity can be expressed with Idiomatic Expressions.

<u>To happen</u> expresses that something is to happen. It is used with fixed personal arrangements or official plans. (Downing – Locke 360)

    e.g. The pope **is to come** to Argentina in February.

    → This is an official plan as it was officially announced some time ago.

<u>To happen</u> can also express "you are (not)". These are orders. (Swan – Walter 140)

    e.g. You **are to make** your homework before you are allowed to play.

    → This is an order.

<u>Be about to</u> (+ infinitive) and <u>be on the point of</u> (+ Gerund) are also ways to express futurity with idiomatic expressions. (Swan – Walter 140)

    e.g. Could you call again tomorrow? We **are just about to leave**.

                                      We **are at the point of leaving**.

    → These are neutral idiomatic expressions.

K. Future in the Past

    When one is talking about the past, one often wants to say that something was still in the future at that time. To emphasise this idea, one can use the **Past Progressive** (formed with was, followed by progressive verb form), **was going to**, **was to** or **would**. (Swan – Walter 141)

    e.g. I **wasn't going to** say anything about the exams, but the students **asked** me to.

    → I had made a fixed plan not to talk about the exams in the past before that past, but afterwards I changed my opinion as the students asked me to.

L. Auxiliaries

Auxiliaries are verbs which have no independent existence as verb phrases, but they help to make up these phrases. The phrase is formed with <u>auxiliary</u> and <u>simple verb form</u>. (Hewings 30-41)

Present Auxiliaries are <u>can, may, will, shall and must</u>.

e.g. We **may/might** come along after breakfast.

→ It is not sure if we come, but we intent to.

Past Auxiliaries are <u>could, might, would and should</u>.

e.g. I **can/could** meet you later.

→ I have the possibility to do it if you want me to.

M. Verb Patterns which express Future

Another way to express futurity are Verb Patterns.

One group of Verb Patterns are <u>is expected, is predicted or is likely</u>. The difference is the intensity of the probability. If something <u>is predicted</u>, there is evidence that it will happen. If it <u>is likely</u>, there is reason to believe that it may happen. If something <u>is expected</u>, it might happen. (Hewings 26)

e.g. Hails of snow **are expected** to continue throughout the night.

→ There is some evidence for this.

Another Verb Pattern is <u>supposed to</u>. It can express an order.

e.g. You **are supposed to** wash the dishes after dinner.

→ You have to do this.

II. Practical Part

In the practical part the rules announced in the theoretical part are described in examples. It will help the comprehension of the sometimes very complex grammatical structures.

If not cited, the examples below are taken from Hewings, Martin: <u>Advanced Grammar in Use</u>.

A. Will and be going to

In this examples the correct future tense and an appropriate verb are required. (Hewings 19)

1. If you press the red button, the machine ....
2. If you listen carefully, you .... an owl in the trees over there.
3. You .... your back if you try to lift that box.
4. If I give you the money .... you .... me some oranges when you're out?

1. In the first example, <u>will start/stop</u> is the correct answer as this is a logical consequence which requires the will future.
2. The second example requires <u>will hear</u> because it is an ability.
3. As the third example is a negative conditional, both <u>will hurt</u> and <u>are going to hurt</u> are possible.
4. The last example is a request. Therefore, <u>will .... buy</u> is the correct answer.

1. A: I can't come over during the day.
   B: I .... you tomorrow evening, then. (see)
2. A: What's the matter with Paula?
   B: She says she .... (be sick)
   A: She .... better with some fresh air. (feel)
3. A: I've been offered a new job in Manchester, so I .... Camco. (leave)
   B: When .... your boss? (tell)
   A: I'm not sure. Perhaps I .... to see him later today. (try)

11

4. A: Did I tell you I .... dinner with Ken on Thursday? (have)

    B: But we .... a film with Ray and Mary on Thursday. You have known about it for weeks. (see)

    A: Sorry. In that case, I .... a different day with Ken. (sort out) (19)

1. As the first example is a decision made at the moment of speaking, <u>will see</u> is the correct answer.
2. <u>Is going to be sick</u> is the correct answer in the second part of the dialogue because it is a prediction based on present evidence. The third part requires <u>will feel</u> because it is a prediction based on opinion and past evidence.
3. In the third dialogue, the first sentence needs <u>am going to leave</u> because the decision is already made. In the second part both concepts are possible. As the speaker is asking about something planned, <u>will you tell</u> *or* <u>are you going to tell</u> are both correct. The last sentence is a decision made at the moment of speaking, which requires <u>will try</u>.
4. The first sentence of the last dialogue insists on <u>am going to have</u> because it is a decision already made in the past. The second part requires <u>are going to see </u>because, as in the sentence before, the decision was already made. The last sentence needs <u>will sort out</u> because the decision was made at the moment of speaking.

B. Present Simple and Present Continuous for the Future

1. We .... our exam results on the 20th August.
2. Jack .... our cats while we are away next week.
3. I think I'll take an umbrella in case it ....
4. There is a reading list to accompany my lecture, while I .... at the end. (21)

1. The first example is a fixed event. <u>Get</u> is the correct answer, but <u>will get</u> is also possible.
2. The next sentence is a less routine arrangement. It requires <u>will look after</u>.
3. With <u>in case</u>, the present simple is required. Therefore, <u>rains</u> is correct.
4. <u>Will give out</u> is demanded because it is a less routine arrangement.

In the next examples, a sentence is given. There are three different answers, whereupon one or two can be correct. Sometimes there is a difference between these two examples. Please explain it. (21)

1. It's not a deep cut, but it .... a scar.
   a. will leave   b. is going to leave   c. is leaving
2. Did you know I .... a new car next week?
   a. will buy   b. am going to buy   c. am buying
3. "I am not sure how I'll get to the concert." "We can take you. We ....
   you up at 8.00."
   a. will pick   b. are going to pick   c. are picking
4. I'm sorry I can't come for dinner. I .... to York tonight. (21)
   a. will driver   b. am going to drive   c. am driving

1. Will leave and is going to leave are the two correct answers in the first example. They have a similar meaning here. Is leaving is incorrect because the prediction is perhaps based on opinion, experience or present evidence.
2. I'm going to buy suggests an intention without a definite arrangement. I'm buying suggests a definite arrangement, because perhaps the speaker has bought the car and is simply picking it up next week. Will buy is the only wrong answer because it is a planned future event.
3. Will pick is the correct answer because it is an offer. Are going to pick and are picking are both incorrect because the decision was made at the point of speaking.
4. In the last example, will drive is incorrect because it is a planned future event. I'm going to drive suggests a personal intention. I'm driving suggests a more definite arrangement. Perhaps the speaker has been told to go there by their employer.

C. Future Continuous and Future Perfect (Continuous)

In the following letter, two alternatives are given. Choose the correct one. (23)

Dear Rosa,

Hope this finds you all well. I suppose by now school (1) *will close/will have closed* for Christmas and you (2) *will be enjoying/will have been enjoying* a rest. It's hard to believe that Tim's already 18 and that it's only a few months until he (3) *will be leaving/will have been leaving* school for college.

My main news is that my brother, John, and his family (4) *will have been arriving/will be arriving* next Friday as part of their big trip around the world. By the time they get here they (5) *will be going/will have been* to California and New Zealand. No doubt John's children (6) *will have been planning/will plan* it all out for months! They (7) *won't be spending/won't have spent* all their time with me. John has to go to Perth on business, so I (8) *will have kept/will be keeping* the rest of the family entertained while he's away. Then they (9) *will all be going/will all have been going* to Sidney [...]

(1) <u>Will have closed</u> is the correct answer because school has closed before the person wrote the letter.

(2) <u>Will be enjoying</u> is appropriate in this example because the holidays are not over yet. The focus is on their duration.

(3) <u>Will be leaving</u> is demanded. The event takes place in the future.

(4) <u>Will be arriving</u> is accurate because next Friday is a clear time indicator that the action did not happen in the past.

(5) <u>Will have been</u> is appropriate. They were in California and in New Zealand before the arrival at the writer's house.

(6) <u>Will have been planning</u> is the right answer because it is the future in the past. They planned it during the last months.

(7) <u>Won't be spending</u> is accurate because the situation didn't start at the time of writing the letter.

(8) <u>Will be keeping</u> is demanded. The focus is on the duration and it neither started nor finished in the past.

(9) <u>Will all be going</u> is the correct answer because they will depart from her home in the future.

D. Weather Forecast

<u>West</u>

The Rockies (1) *will continue* to add to their snow pack as more Pacific systems ride through the region on Friday.

Snow (2) *will hang* on across southeast Colorado and eastern New Mexico on Saturday as low pressure (3) *develops* over the southern Plains and (4) *begins* to track north-eastward away from the region.

The next Pacific storm (5) *will launch* an assault on the Pacific Northwest on Saturday. Rain (6) *will be* on the increase from western Washington to northwest California with snow levels ranging from 2000 feet in the Washington Cascades to 4500 feet in the Siskiyou and northern Sierra.

Another Pacific storm (7) *will arrive* on the Northwest Coast by Sunday night.

<u>Midwest</u>

Stagnant air with low level moisture and a snow cover has brought dense fog, drizzle and freezing drizzle over the heart of the Midwest. (8) You*'ll need to use* big caution travelling in this region with expected delays on the ground and at airports through about noon. High temperatures (9) *will range* from the upper teens and 20s in North Dakota to the 50s and low 60s in southern Missouri and Kentucky.

The weekend (10) *will feature* a significant storm across most of the region. The storm (11) *will move* quickly out of the southern Plains early on Saturday and (12) *will intensify* near the Great Lakes on Saturday night. Mild air (13) *will move up* ahead of a cold front so some areas that saw snow last weekend (14) *will see* rain this time. Colder air rushing in behind the front (15) *will change* rain to freezing rain, sleet and then snow.

On Saturday, a 2-to-4-inch band of snow (16) *will extend* from Kansas to Minnesota. Saturday night into Sunday morning, a heavier band of snow (17) *may set up* from the Missouri-Illinois line to Wisconsin, Upper Michigan and western Lower Michigan where accumulations (18) *could locally reach* 6 inches.

Chicago and Milwaukee (19) *may see* 3 or 4 inches of snow overnight as temperatures tumble. Roads across the Midwest (20) *may turn* icy on Saturday night as water (21) *freezes* and snow fall on top. The storm (22) *will turn* very windy Saturday night and Sunday. Gusts (23) *could reach* 35 to 50 mph over the western Great Lakes Sunday.

This passage has been taken from
<http://www.weather.com/newscenter/fcstsummary.html?from=wxcenter_news>
on 22nd December 2007

This is a weather forecast, and therefore the correct time concept used is the will future, although there are some exceptions. In (3) and (4), Present Simple is used. It gives the reason for the future happening and is thus a fact. Some verbs, like (17), (18), (19), (20) and (23), have auxiliaries to express the possibility of the event. Example (21) is in Present Simple because it is a law of nature that water freezes at 0°C or lower.

E. Newspaper Article

The finding (1) *could apply* to other planets in the solar system which have condensable atmospheres like Mars, or even to extra sola- planets, Gurwell told SPACE.com.

In the future, Gurwell (2) *hopes* that astronomers (3) *will be able* to make even more precise measurements of Pluto using the Atacama Large Millimeter Array (ALMA) currently being built in Chile. The ALMA is scheduled for completion in 2012 but early scientific experiments (4) *could begin* as soon as 2008.

Gurwell (5) *expects* that the ALMA (6) *will allow* astronomers to see where on Pluto's surface nitrogen gas (7) *is being generated* and whether the atmosphere is spread out evenly across the entire planet or concentrated in hot spot like on Saturn's moon, Enceladus.

This passage has been taken from
<http://www.cnn.com/2006/TECH/space/01/03/pluto.temp/index.html>
on 22nd December 2007

(1) In the first example, an auxiliary verb is used to express possibility.

(2) The Present Simple is utilised in this sentence because a time indicator is used.

(3) The will future is demanded because the speaker talks about his personal hopes.

(4) An auxiliary is used in this example because it expresses the possibility of a future happening.

(5) The verb in this sentence expresses a future wish.

(6) The will future is demanded because a wish or a hope is expressed.

(7) The Future Continuous is used because the writer talks about a fixed future plan. It is also a passive verb construction.

III. Conclusion

This work should have put emphasis on the various uses of the future concepts. The theoretical part is extended with examples as they should serve a better understanding. The texts are written in an advanced level of language. This should be helpful for daily use.

As this topic is very complex, this paper should serve as an overview. For a more detailed analysis, Grammar Books, like Downing and Locke, should be consulted.

IV. Bibliography

List of works cited

Downing, Angela and Philip Locke. <u>English Grammar – A University Course</u>. 2. ed. London and New York: Routledge Taylor & Francis Group, 2006.

Hewings, Martin. <u>Advanced Grammar in Use</u>. 2. ed. Cambridge: Cambridge University Press, 2005.

Swan, Michael and Catherine Walter. <u>How English Works – A Grammar Practice Book</u>. 14. ed. Oxford: Oxford University Press, 2004.

Text extracts

Than, Ker. "Astronomers: Pluto Colder Than Expected." Cable News Networks. 2007. 22 Dec. 2007 <http://www.cnn.com/2006/TECH/space/01/03/pluto.temp/index.html>.

"Future Tense." <u>wikipedia.org.</u> 2007. 22 Dec. 2007 <http://en.wikipedia.org/wiki/Future_tense>.

"Weather Forecast." <u>weather.com</u> 2007. 22 Dec. 2007 <http://www.weather.com/newscenter/fcstsummary.html?from=wxcenter_news>.